MW01205012

IAMZUMN

By

Brian T. Summerson

Building a great life…..one day at a time

First Iamzumn Publications Edition, July 2006

Copyright © by Brian T. Summerson

All rights reserved under International and
Pan-American Copyright Conventions.
Published in the United States by
Iamzumn Publishing

This book is protected in whole, in part, or in any form under the Copyright
Laws of the United States of America, The British Empire, including the
Dominion of Canada, and all other countries of the Copyright Union.
All Rights, including professional, amateur, motion picture, recitation, radio,
television, and public reading, are strictly reserved

Summerson, Brian T.
IAMZUMN- first edition
An Iamzumn Publication
ISBN 0-9788942-0-0
Printed in the United States of America

Dedication

To my wife Karen and my son Brian Jordan, may we build a great life together… one day at a time.

FORWARD

As a child, I was a fast-paced towhead busy doing all day long whatever I thought of doing. A constant flow of questions was always a part of my daily routine. Thirty-something years later, I can say that the more I experience, learn, and live, the more my appetite for living has increased.

I believe that you can capture an idea from any book you read that will make you think how to make your life better. Some people like to use the analogy of the combination lock. Where you are in life can be compared to the numbers on a combination lock. Each new experience or idea has helped to align the numbers. However, there is that last one or two numbers of the lock's combination that needs to be identified in order to unlock the next level of success in your life. Then the process starts all over again.

The goal in writing this book is to share part of my story and experiences, to build an emotional attachment to the idea of breaking the habit of living from one paycheck to the next paycheck while simultaneously delivering the message of personal development in harmony with a team of people that will assist you in all areas of life.

It is a fact that everyone is affected by other people's actions. The Sept.11, 2001 actions of a few have affected our lives forever.

How you live your life does matter. The decisions that you make on a daily basis do:

- create the future – good, bad, positive or negative
- affect your family and love ones
- can help you or harm you
- will produce financial success or the constant challenge of living day to day

It is your choice. God has given you gifts and talents. What are you going to do to make a difference in your world? Life is not easy and you cannot control most circumstances. But those you can control will determine your future.

If I can inspire one person to rise above, to build a better lifestyle, and produce a quality of life that builds better families, businesses, cities and nations, the journey will have been worth it.

WILL YOU BE THE ONE?

TABLE OF CONTENTS

CHAPTER 1: THE DAY HAS FINALLY COME:
"ENOUGH IS ENOUGH!"

The day has finally come after waiting eight months to take the annual vacation. Fifteen years of working has earned Frequent Flyer Frank three weeks of vacation each year. His bags are packed, the family is piled into the SUV and they are off to the airport for two weeks in Florida that was paid in advance on his credit card. The bad news is that he doesn't know where the money is going to come from; the good news is he will get an additional 4,500 frequent-flyer miles!

Off to the airport. There are many last-minute items Frequent Flyer Frank and his wife Cautious Kate take care of during their 20-minute drive to the airport. Cautious Kate makes three phone calls from her cell phone. There was a voice-mail message to call Betty Banker, their local branch banker, after 9 a.m. It is 9:05 and she calls. They are five minutes from the airport and are right on time, leaving two hours before their flight for check-in. The children are in a great mood. Cautious Kate is very excited to be going to Florida.   Kate has worked for eight months without a vacation and desperately needs a break from her routine.

"Betty Banker," Cautious Kate says, "I am following up with your voice mail from last evening." Then Betty Banker proceeds to tell Cautious Kate that the checking account was overdrawn by $858 and this issue needs to be taken care of immediately. "Eight hundred and fifty eight dollars," Cautious Kate yells...how can that be?

There is dead silence in the SUV. Suddenly Cautious Kate begins to cry, trying to hold back the emotion and not let the children know that there is a problem – a very big problem. She hangs up. Cautious Kate turns and looks at Frequent Flyer Frank, "We are overdrawn on our checking account by $858 and there is only $275 dollars in the savings account."

Suddenly Frequent Flyer Frank snaps out of the trance he was in when the policeman behind him at the airport blows his horn. He thought he took care of everything. How can this be?

It turns out that their annual premium for their life insurance appeared on their bank account as a $1,058 automatic withdrawal yesterday after they had withdrawn $630 cash for the vacation. He thought that the $300 would cover everything until his semi-monthly paycheck was deposited in their bank account in five days.

Unloading the luggage Frequent Flyer Frank's mind is racing. Why does it always happen to me? The children yell, "Hurry up, Dad!" Cautious Kate is now stressed because of the overdraw issue and now it is time to check in at the Northwest counter for their two-week vacation. They walk into the airport and see a check-in line of more than 200 people. Early this morning the National Terrorist Alert was raised to orange. It normally is not a problem except that a man had been arrested earlier that day after trying to get past the magnetometer with a loaded pistol.

Now they are waiting in line thinking about how to rectify the overdrawn balance in their checking account. Reaching for his cell phone Frequent Flyer Frank says, "I have an idea that will buy us time." After dialing Betty Banker's phone number, he gets her voice mail. "Hello, Betty Banker, this is Frequent Flyer Frank. I am sorry about any overdraft on my account. It was an oversight on my part, missing the annual life-insurance payment. I am at the airport getting ready to fly to Florida. We should arrive at 12:35 p.m. I plan to make an electronic payment into our account this afternoon. Is there any way to increase the overdraft protection to $1,000 or $1,500? Thanks for understanding. Call me on my cell phone at 210-123-4567 to confirm the receipt of the deposit. Goodbye."

"Next," calls the voice from behind the counter. Cautious Kate looks at Frequent Flyer Frank and mutters "How are we going to make a deposit?"

On the way to the gate he explains to Cautious Kate that they have a credit line of $7,500 and they have used $4,500 of it to buy the vacation. He will get a cash advance of $1,000 to cover the negative balance. "More borrowing," Cautious Kate says. He looks in Cautious Kate's eyes and he sees tears and he feels her emotion. His gut is tight and now Frequent Flyer Frank's mind is racing and trying to figure out how he will pay back the money he has just borrowed and got stuck with another $1,000 on the credit card.

Displaying his frustration, Frequent Flyer Frank yells out, "When will this end? I work so hard and I can't seem to get ahead.

Enough is Enough!"

CHAPTER 2: EVERYONE HAS A PHILOSOPHY
FOR LIVING:
"WHAT HAVE YOU ADOPTED"

Everyone has a philosophy of living life whether he/she knows it or not. Those who take the time to understand what philosophy they are embracing can become empowered to change their philosophies to create better circumstances in their lives.

In my opinion, there is a way to live your life so that you can be successful day in and day out. What you expect determines how successful you will be. If you expect perfection, you always will fail in this world. However, if you expect excellence in the context of living a life of balance, your thoughts and actions will be guided in life by the framework of that philosophy. That framework increases the potential to be a successful person in each phase of your life.   Zig Ziglar's motto, as recorded on his website www.zigziglar.com under Zig Ziglar Bio, states "you can have everything in life you want if you will just help enough other people get what they want." What is your philosophy of living? Jim Rohn has an audio series, the Philosophy of

Living. Listening to this will prompt you to ask yourself the question, "What is really my philosophy?"

Your decision-making process is affected by the philosophy of the living you choose. The method in which you gather information and ideas, and how you synthesize them to make decisions, becomes the foundation of your life. The better you become in developing this skill, the more successful you will be, and the better your life will become. How do I know if I am making good decisions? Reflect on your life and see what your track record shows. If over the last 10 years you have spent your time becoming an expert watching all of the television episodes of "Friends" instead of participating in your child's life, we can safely say that you could have made a better decision. To further that, instead of watching other people getting paid to do what they love at the expense of your time, begin today spending that same half hour per week for the next 10 years thinking of ideas that can help you and your family financially. Thirty minutes per week, 52 weeks a year for 10 years is 260 hours (six-and-a-half working weeks). Do you think if you search for six-and-a-half working weeks you might find the answer to assist you in becoming financially literate? By replacing the old habit of watching TV with the new habit of using your brain to identify ideas to help you financially, the chances are extremely good that you will be further ahead financially.

If you are in need of brushing up on your decision-making skills, I urge you to purchase the book "<u>The Confidential Decision Maker</u>" by Roger Dawson and study and apply the lessons. Also, remember what I wrote in the Forward:

How you live your life does matter. The decisions that you make on a daily basis do:

- create the future – good, bad, positive or negative
- affect your family and love ones
- can help you or harm you
- will produce financial success or the constant challenge of living day to day

It is your choice.

More watching
than reading

Average amount of time 8-to
18 year olds spend daily:

Watching
TV   **3 hours, 51 min.**

Listening to
music   **1 hour, 44 min.**

Using a
computer   **1 hour, 2 min.**

Playing
video games   **49 min.**

Reading   **43 min.**

Watching
movies   **25 min.**

Source: USA Today, March 10, 2005, *Electronic world swallows up kids' time, study finds (Marilyn Elias)*

CHAPTER 3: MY $300,000 MBA
LEARNING BY DOING THINGS RIGHT AND DOING THINGS WRONG

The Story of Dura Task Corporation

As an entrepreneur one has an intense desire to create. The more one becomes successful, the more creation becomes an extension of the ego. I first learned of this concept during a meeting with Tom Handwork, my estate attorney. As far as egos go, when it comes to learning to manage appropriately, I am sure that people around me have noticed that I am a dedicated perfectionist.

During my early years as a bookkeeper at Dura Temp Corporation, I felt a need to help other small-business owners provide services in the newly-emerging DOT COM era. After contemplating this business idea for years, I felt that it was time to start my dream company and bring it to fruition. In early 1998, I was just becoming better acquainted with Dave Rollins and his family through church activities. During one of our "small-group" evenings, I was in charge of ordering and picking up the pizza for a special activity. I asked Dave to accompany me to Little Caesars Pizza shop.

As we entered the establishment, without hesitation Dave blurted out his assessment of the current status of Little Caesars pizza shop – personnel, orders, overhead, etc. I was impressed. I thought about that evening more than 100 times and thought that Dave is someone I wanted on my team; my new start-up team.

The day came about six months later when I made the final decision to commence with this new project. After approximately two weeks of business travel visiting customers in Australia, and some rest and relaxation in Waikiki, I made the decision during the return flight home that "this is now or never." Then I committed myself to start the journey. Upon arrival home, I made a dinner appointment with Dave Rollins. During dinner at Applebee's my proposal to start a business to support small business owners changed our lives. Through our discussion we had become energized and I had finally stopped wishing and started living the dream.

So many things to do, so little time to do them. Not only was I managing the growth of Dura Temp Corporation, my energy now was going to be divided and used for another dream. Adding more responsibility created more energy with the challenge to GET IT ALL DONE! Note: I was crazy enough to start two other small businesses at the same time…. can we say EGO!

Dura Task Corporation was formed for the purpose of providing Internet consulting and Web-page designing. With Dave's experience in supporting entrepreneurs and human-resource management, coupled with my business experience and "deep pockets of money," we were in business.

The DOT COM boom was on and we were caught up in it. Especially since cash was not an issue at the time of the start-up. It was a thrill to create a new entity. Starting with Dave and me working out of my house, we hired a computer programmer and began marketing the Internet and Web Page-consulting services. The needs were great so we decided to move out of my house and into a small 500-square-foot second-story office in Maumee, Ohio. An administrative assistant and graphic designer were hired. Dave and the crew built a customer base, which produced a lot of activity for our service. Constant communication between Dave and me became a very high priority. The business goal was within reach and we were learning to understand both sides of being business owners. With our short history, some potential customers elected not to use us as their Internet support even though we had the best price and could fulfill the customer's expectations.

The needs were great so we decided to expand our work force even though Dura Task was not generating a profit. (We took a chance on the possibility of getting the "big customer" instead of focusing on becoming profitable with the "small-customer" business). This was a mistake and was founded in the abundance of available cash. We landed the "big customer" and began working on a website to facilitate his 60,000-plus customers. There were project delays and contract issues associated with this project. Our decision to go for the big customer (ego again) was ill-fated and created a money-losing venture we had to stop. With this disaster and lack of ability to generate a positive cash flow, the business was closed at the end of August 2000. I ended up losing hundreds of thousands of dollars and was left with more than $280,000 in debt (repaid over a period of time). *This was a stressful learning experience!*

Would I do it over again? Yes! I experienced so many new things, met new people and participated in a dream I had pondered for years. Analyzing every aspect of the experience, I realized I had also learned a lot, such as: Start small and generate a positive cash flow as soon a possible (very basic to a company's success).

Too much seed capital can be dangerous to the health of an organization. It can lull you into a false sense of security if the company is not generating cash. The Dot Com burn rate of cash is what Dura Task experienced.

As an entrepreneur who has experienced a business failing, a loss can be devastating. However, keep pushing on through your doubts, depression, and loss of confidence. As an entrepreneur, you can try again. It is okay not to be perfect or have a perfect experience. The most important point is being true to yourself and give your best.

Blame. You can not blame others for your predicament. The responsibility is yours. Deal with it and move on to the next project. By moving on, the healing begins.

Don't co-sign for anything.

Be up front with your expectations. Identify all the risks and know what the failure rate is. I was fortunate that, during the initial dinner meeting with Dave Rollins, I stated that: "before you commit to do this start-up, that no matter what, we are friends. Business is business, but we cannot lose our friendship over this." I am happy to report that we didn't lose our friendship. In 2005, Dave went on to become president of one of my companies – Dura Temp Corporation.

Know your entrepreneurial style. (More on that in Chapter 5)

A closing note to this chapter. This experience has many positive aspects. Dave and I have personally and pro-fessionally been stretched and have entrenched the entrepre-neurial spirit even deeper in our souls. In May 2001, I lis-tened to the Rich Dad Poor Dad book on cassette by Robert T. Kiyosaki. I was inspired that I was already doing what he ascribes. Dave Rollins also listened to the tape and it dra-matically changed his prior thinking, that of "getting a job and working hard all your life will be enough". **That is not enough**. You must do more.

CHAPTER 4: READING

"YOU HAVE THE TIME TO READ"

"Too many books, not enough time" has been a phase I have heard and said over and over. I am fascinated with the challenge to read all that I can; and listen to good books all that I can.

Several years ago, I attended a Jim Rohn two-day seminar (plus a third-day master mind session). One of his special guest speakers was Charlie "Tremendous" Jones. Charlie articulated his passion in his speech with his famous statement, "You are the same today (that) you will be in five years except for two things, the people you meet and the books you read." A great way to meet people is through the books they have written. I had the privilege to be exposed to great thinkers through audio programs from the Nightingale-Conant Corporation. My father gave me the opportunity to be exposed to people like Earl Nightingale, Jim Rohn, Dennis Waitley, Zig Ziglar, Napoleon Hill, and Brian Tracy.

Sometimes my father and I would listen to them in the car; other times we would listen to them while we worked on a project together. Listening to books on cassette tapes was a way that gave me the resource to tap into other minds to help me develop and grow as a person. An even greater benefit was that listening served as the bridge that gave me the decision to read books and overcome the slow-reading problem I had. I am hooked. I now love books.

Are you constantly reading? If you don't take time to read daily, you are missing the opportunity to improve your life which will take you in a new direction. Jim Rohn said "the books you don't read won't help." I will go even further; the choice to not read on a daily basis eliminates you from being better prepared to receive life-changing ideas. Those who do read will not miss that opportunity.

My son Brian J. (age 9 at the time) had developed into a voracious reader and was participating in the acceler-ated-reading program at school. My wife Karen, who has done an excellent job, and I spent years reading to him, expanding his vocabulary, and challenging to him to read books. He decided to read J.K. Rowling's book Harry Potter and the Sorcerer's Stone. During the course of reading this book, Brian J. would share some events that Harry Potter experienced. I developed interest enough to read the book. Big dilemma: how can I find time to read all the Harry Potter books plus read the books currently on my list to read, let alone the stack of unread books which I want to read? Too many books, not enough time is always the case. My compelling interest and desire to read these books, led me to delegate the commute time back and forth to work for this experience. Off I went to the library to check out the first Harry Potter book on cassette and began my journey into the world of Harry Potter.

Using my automobile as a learning center has been a lifestyle for the last 18 years. But this was different...
Shortly after I began listening to Harry Potter and the Sorcerer's Stone, I became fascinated and enthralled by the story (Jim Dale is an exceptional reader). Some nights I couldn't wait to get home and chat with my son about a particular event in the book. One evening during a chat, I got the idea to challenge Brian J. to read all the books in the series. He agreed and the contract was signed on Jan. 14, 2001:

The following agreement is between Brian T.

Summerson and Brian Jordan Summerson.

It is agreed that Brian will buy one electronic game (or approved equivalent option) for Brian Jordan when the following books are read:

Harry Potter and the Sorcerer's Stone

Harry Potter and the Chamber of Secrets

Harry Potter and the Prisoner of Azkaban

Harry Potter and the Goblet of Fire

This agreement will be effective until June 1, 2001. I didn't realize what unexpected benefits would result from this agreement.

Three-and-a-half months later, we completed the books. Brian J. read the four books with comprehension and went on to be the top accelerated reader in the third grade. We had bonded through the experiences in the books by chatting together (spending time). Brian J. on his own reinforced the goal-setting process and learned how to overcome what he first thought was a difficult objective. For me, I completed all the Harry Potter books I would otherwise have not read; and even participated in Brian Jordan's school project. And, yes, he purchased his electronic game.

What an experience! The decision to "read" the books created an awesome opportunity to interact with my son. I'm glad I didn't miss this opportunity to bond with him.

Read all the books; listen to all the audio tapes or CD's. What life-changing ideas will you come across? It is a choice to read. Minutes a day can change your life, make you a better person, parent, leader or employee in your organization. And remember, share the insights from the books you have read. Tell a friend about a book that may help him. I was taught that books are my friends and I would always learn something from every book. And believe me, the last 20 years of pouring good ideas into my mind has paid many dividends both personally and professionally.

Here is a brief list of books I think are worth reading:

The Bible

Think and Grow Rich – Napoleon Hill

The Richest Man in Babylon – George S. Clason

21 Laws of Leadership; John C. Maxwell

The Millionaire Maker – Loral Langemeier

Thomas Jefferson – A Life – William Sterne Randall

Leading an Inspired Life - Jim Rohn

One Year Off – David Elliot Cohen

The Psychology of Winning – Dennis Waitley

The Millionaire Next Door - Thomas J. Stanley, PH D., William D. Danko, PH D.

Rich Dad Poor Dad – Robert Kiyosaki

Good to Great – Jim Collins

The Sales Bible – Jeffery H. Gitomer

Joining the Entrepreneurial Elite – Olaf Isachsen

Snoopy's Guide to the Writing of Life – Barnaby Conrad and Monte Schultz

The Seven Habits of Highly Effective People – Steven Covey

Here is a brief list of other authors – I encourage people to read their books:

Brian Tracy

Ken Blanchard

Zig Ziglar

Mark H. McCormak

Harvey MacKay

Tom Peters

Earl Nightingale

Larry Barkett

Roger Dawson

CHAPTER 5: STARTING POINT -
SEVEN STRATEGIES TO PREPARE FOR
FINANCIAL SUCCESS

Before you can leave "living paycheck to paycheck," you must consider one main thing:

Believe and *commit to the idea that you can leave living paycheck to paycheck* (and even far beyond). It is the <u>belief that you can</u> that will carry you through. The rest is a mechanical process that can be duplicated.

Rule #1: Grab hold of the belief to spend less than you earn. You don't have to have everything right now. Learn to delay gratification (which goes counter to our culture's way of thinking). Think of ways to leverage your money.

Rule #2: Identify your distractions; and then control them. Remember how you manage your money is based on a philosophy. Transfer your thinking and focus on a new set of behaviors. There always will be more wants, which is the dilemma. It is not about the wants, it is about your control of yourself to manage your resources versus giving into the wants.

Rule #3: Get to know yourself! Your thought process is the key to your future success. Why do you do what you do? Identify your personality and your entrepreneurial style.

Embracing rule number three, "Get to know yourself" will be a challenge. The way you deal with yourself is an education in itself. There are many resources that can help, and I will give you three. First, Florence Littauer in her book Personality Plus identifies personalities. The study of personalities is fascinating and by knowing what type you are versus what types other people are, you can begin a more effective form of communication with others. Second, Jerry Clark has an audio series, "What is Your Color?" that embraces what Florence Littauer has done but uses colors instead of the technical applications. And third, Olaf Isachsen's *Joining the Entrepreneurial Elite* is an outstanding book that identifies the personalities of entrepreneurs. I met Olaf in 2000, and through a course of a few conversations he gave me copies of two of his books, one being *Joining the Entrepreneurial Elite.*

Months after receiving the book, I chose to read it during a Northwest flight from Detroit to San Juan, Puerto Rico. My wife Karen was traveling with me, and as usual we read books on the airplane. However, this flight would change my life forever. Eagar to get into the book, I began reading. Then, there it was in black and white, a detailed description of my thought-process style – I am a **Strategist!** I quickly began reading it to my wife and was laughing almost to tears over each sentence **describing me! What insight!**

Joining the Entrepreneurial Elite discusses four types of entrepreneurs: the Administrator, the Tactician, the Strategist, and the Idealist. On page 9 of his book, Isachsen summarizes the personality temperaments, citing the work of Jung, Briggs, Myers, and David Keirsey:

Administrator – A concrete affiliate or what Jung called a *sensing-judging* person. You rely upon your senses and you organize by exercising judgments.

Tactician – A concrete pragmatist or what may be called a *sensing-perceiver.* You gather information through your senses and organize it through your perceptive preferences.

Strategist – An abstract pragmatist or what may be called an *intuitive-thinker.* In other words, you rely upon your ability to reason combined with the use of your intuition.

Idealist – An abstract-affiliate or what may be called an *intuitive feeler.* You rely upon your values and intuition.

Knowing that I am wired as a strategist explains a lot of why and how I do what I do. Having this knowledge gives me more power to effectively manage my businesses and personal life. Putting this knowledge to use by having an administrator-type person run my company and a tactician for my CFO as a part of my team, has greatly helped to communicate with other members of my organization and get the business of the day completed. A quick note: I am an adult with ADD (Attention Deficit Disorder). Coupling ADD with the strategies-type of entrepreneurial style can be frustrating to my organization as well as exciting. Their biggest challenge is to find out what Brian is thinking and what his next move will be. In the early days of my business career, I was not as effective as a leader because I lacked the knowledge and understanding of the entrepreneurial types. Thanks, Olaf, for taking the time to share your book. It has changed my life.

(To order *Joining the Entrepreneurial Elite*, go to www.iamzumn.com)

Rule #4: Do your financial bookkeeping – How much money do you have? How much do you owe? This will be painful. There are plenty of books that will take you through this process. Remember this is a process that takes time and effort. But it must be done and there are no short cuts. If you are overwhelmed – **Get some help!** Your object is to control it, not to avoid it simply because there isn't enough money.

Refer to a list of books and website www.iamzumn .com

Rule #5: In his audio series Anthony Robbins gives

us the **Ultimate Success Formula:**

1. Know your goal (What do you want?) Clarity of what you want is power.

2. Know why you want it. (Purpose) Reasons come first; answers come second.

3. Take massive action. What stops people from taking action? Fear.

4. Know what you are getting.

5. Change your approach **until** you become financially successful.

It is hard to improve the Ultimate Success Formula. Until now, you have managed your financial decisions, which have produced results (whether you like the results or not.) The great news is, by following the fifth step in this formula – you can, **you can,** *YOU CAN!* Change your approach until you become financially successful.

Rule #6: Don't just work for a paycheck. Get meaning out of your life. You have an awesome responsibility to manage your life. God has given you gifts and talents to be used. If you haven't thought about it lately, what are your God-given gifts and talents? How can you develop your life, and **live it daily,** to use these God-given gifts to make not only your life better, but for those around you? Remember to build upon your **strengths.**

Rule #7: Find a mentor. I have been very fortunate to have had mentors in my life; including being mentored through books. Loral Langemeier has a program called Loral's Big Table (I currently am in number 20). She has a philosophy that all millionaires are team-made millionaires. In my experiences, I have found that to be true.

Rule #8: Change your thinking about money and focus on creative ways through ideas to increase the amount of money that will come to you. For example, Robert Kiyosaki, author of *Rich Dad Poor Dad*, teaches us to ask the question, "How can I afford it?" as opposed to "I can't afford it."

CHAPTER 6: IDEAS

"A FORMULA FOR WEALTH"

As I mentioned in a previous chapter, I am participating in Loral Langemeier's "Loral's Big Table #20." This group has come together to find out how to play a bigger, better financial game. Some of the participants are earning their money in the W2 mode (they derive their income only from their jobs). Other participants have money, resources, multiple companies, and investment strategies. And still others are identified somewhere in between the first two categories.

The Loral's Big Table was built upon the philosophy to act, think, and make money the way the wealthy do. Loral's book, The Millionaire Maker, has brilliantly articulated the wealth process and I urge you to purchase a copy of her book ASAP. Read it. Study it. Then **Go Do The Work** by Leading your Wealth Program. For the last 20 years I have struggled to figure out the wealth-building process. Loral's book provides you with an excellent mentor resource.

There are many vehicles and roads to wealth. It is

your job to believe in yourself and have the faith that you can do it. The process of getting wealthy takes time. Enjoy the process!

CHAPTER 7: AROUND THE WORLD:
"MENTORING BY A FATHER"

The best way to mentor people thoroughly is to have the student observe the mentor for an extended period of time. Through this exercise, the mentor must participate in the experience; and through repetition, his or her student matures and grows into a master.

This symbiotic relationship is beneficial not only to the student, but also to the teacher. One of the best ways to learn something is to teach it. There's no better way to transition into this chapter.

There are, as the saying goes, "people who make things happen, there are people who watch things happen, and there are people who wonder what happens." One of the goals in this book is to <u>encourage you to become a person who thinks and makes things happen</u>.

The following is an account of my trip around the world in March 2005. I used this trip as a vehicle to mentor my son Brian J. I would like to share with you, the reader, insight into the paralleled thinking this process uses to become successful in any adventure.

Purpose

To meet with existing customers in their country to assess the current status of their hot-glass-handling needs; and to determine how I can help them in the future.

To mentor Brian J. in aspects of international business with a global hands-on experience.

To successfully transfer fundamentals of business and relationships by setting the best example I can and to prepare him to meet the challenges of the future.

To become educated in the different cultures of the world.

Agenda

As you will read in the coming pages, everyone has an agenda. If you don't create your agenda you will be following someone else's agenda which may have harmful consequences. Be careful to know what you really want.

Preparation

In preparation for a trip around the world, one must have a clear set of goals. These goals should be specific, achievable, and dated. The better you prepare the greater chance of a successful outcome.

Organization

Great organization is a prerequisite for effective use of your time and emotional welfare. The effective management of time, people, money, ideas, information and plans, are key determiners of how and when you are successful. If your organizational skills are just okay, find someone who has great organizational skills and become a team. The level of achievement and time saved will be enormous as the years pass.

Team Effort

In order to work effectively in this world you will have to be comfortable working with people and developing your people skills. Those who take this to heart have a greater chance of big success. The kind of person you are does matter in the market place and it is best if you understand yourself. Effective communication with people is how this is done.

In order to complete a trip around the world you have to enlist hundreds of teams, directly or indirectly, such as teams at the airlines, hotels, taxi cab companies, restaurants, banks, customers, communities, local governments, and country governments. Having hundreds, if not thousands, of people working together and performing the services in a team fashion is vital. We depend on these teams to work. Effective communication is paramount especially when there is a language barrier. I have found that people's needs are basically the same and a smile and a pleasing demeanor go a long way in communication with people.

Relationships

Good relationships in business are everything.

Expenses

Spending money should have a purpose. Those who understand value, have a better long-term outcome. The value of meeting customers face to face can prove to be extremely valuable not only economically, but socially as well.

Rule: Always spend less than you earn (most people break this rule).

Implementation

Now that we have our purpose and agenda, and we are sufficiently prepared, it is time for implementation. This step can be the most exciting. Note: Even the best plans can be subject to change. If you are prepared, you can respond with flexibility (which is the best policy when traveling internationally.)

AROUND THE WORLD TRIP

March 2005

Brian T. Summerson

Brian J. Summerson

Thursday, March 10, 2005

4:30 p.m. – Limousine service to Detroit International Airport

5:00 p.m. – Check bags and Check-in

7:00 p.m. – NW Flight 54

      Depart DTW

Friday, March 11, 2005

9:00 a.m. – Arrive Amsterdam

2:30 p.m. – Flight NW8371/KL427 Depart Amsterdam

11:45 p.m. – Arrive Dubai

Taxi to the Sheraton Deira Hotel & Towers

Saturday, March 12, 2005

Sightseeing in Dubai (and time-zone adjustment)

Sunday, March 13, 2005

10:30 a.m. – Meeting at Al Tajir Glass

Monday, March 14, 2005

Sightseeing in Dubai (day was reserved for additional business if required)

Tuesday, March 15, 2005

12:00 noon – Check-in at Dubai Airport (DBX)

2:00 p.m. – Flight DK3512 Depart Dubai

6:30p p.m. – Arrive Delhi (DEL)

Taxi to ITC Hotel Maurya Sheraton & Towers

Meet Dura Temp's Sales Representative

Wednesday, March 16, 2005

Morning – To Agra to see the Taj Mahal and Gatehpur Sikri

Afternoon – Drive to Jaipur

Evening – Hotel The Haveli (Old Indian Palace)

Thursday, March 17, 2005

Morning – Excursion to Amber Fort & Elephant Ride

Afternoon – Tour city of Jaipur, aka "Pink City"

Evening – Return to Delhi - ITC Hotel Maurya Sheraton & Towers

Brian and Brian J. First Class NWA

Brian and Brian J. in Dubai, UAE, Jumeriah Beach - with Burj Al Arab in the background

Brian and Brian J. preparing to go to work

Brian and Brian J. taking in some of the culture

Dura Temp Corporation Representative for India:
Brian J. , Jay Sarin, Divya Sarin, Brian

Amber Fort,
India

Luxury
Resort in
Dubai with
Burj Al Arab
in the
background

Successful trip - saying goodbye

India Gate - Delhi, India

Brian and Brian J. on an
Elephant ride to
Amber Fort, India

Arrival in Manila,
Phillippines

Petronas Towers - Kuala Lumpur
Malaysia

Corregidor Island, Philippines - Summersons and Brunks
soaking up history

Malinta
Tunnel -
Corregidor
Island

Corregidor Island, Philippines - General Douglas MacArthur
"I shall return"

Meeting held in Tokyo, Japan with Chiyoda Trading Corporation Staff

Chiyoda
Trading
Corporation
Tokyo
Office

Tokyo -
Dave
Rollins,
Brian T.
Summerson,
Mr. Suzaki

Tokyo - Dave Rollins, Brian T. Summerson, Brian J. Summerson, Mr. Seki

Hard Rock Cafe - Osaka

Dinner with Chiyoda trading Corporation Osaka branch staff

Karen Summerson, Brian J. Summerson, Mr. Aka Matsu Ko Ji

Brian J. Summerson with Mr. Masaya Dogan from the Osaka branch

Lunch in Osaka, Japan

Osaka, Japan Dontonbori

Brian J. Summerson, Mr. Ala Matsu Ko Ji

Friday, March 18, 2005

Morning - Visit HNG (hot glass handling customer)

Dinner with Dura Temp's Representative

9:10 p.m. – Check in at Delhi International Airport

11:10 p.m. – Flight MH191 Depart Delhi

Saturday, March 19, 2005

7:00 a.m. – Arrive in Kuala Lumpur

Take the Express Train to Hilton Kuala Lumpur

Travel Layover

Afternoon – Sightseeing

Sunday, March 20, 2005

8:30 a.m. – Taxi to airport

9:20 a.m. – Check-in

11:20 a.m. – Flight MN704 Depart Kuala Lumpur

3:15 p.m. – Arrive Manila, Philippines

Stay with the Brunk Family (missionaries)

Monday, March 21, 2005

Staying with the Brunk Family

Visit Corregidor Island in Philippines

Tuesday, March 22, 2005

8:30 a.m. – Taxi to Asia Brewery

11:00 a.m. – Meeting at Asia Brewery (hot glass handling customer)

Taxi to the Westin Philippine Plaza

Wednesday, March 23, 2005

6:00 a.m. – Taxi to airport

6:20 a.m. – Check-in

8:20 a.m. – Flight NW20 Depart Manila

1:10 p.m. – Arrive Tokyo

Karen Summerson and Dave Rollins (Dura Temp Corp.'s VP) arrive (March 22)

Check-in the Westin Tokyo

Evening – Dinner with Chiyoda Trading Corp. (Tokyo Staff)

Thursday, March 24, 2005

Morning – Meeting at Chiyoda Trading Corp. office (representatives of Dura Temp)

Afternoon/Evening – Sightseeing in Tokyo

Friday, March 25, 2005

Morning – Take the Bullet Train to Kyoto; meet Mr. Dogan

Westin Miyako Kyoto

Saturday, March 26, 2005

Sightseeing in Kyoto

Travel to Osaka; Hard Rock Café

Sunday, March 27, 2005

Morning/Afternoon – Sightseeing in Osaka

Evening – Dinner with Chiyoda Trading Corp. (Osaka Staff)

Monday, March 28, 2005

Morning – Meet with Chiyoda Trading Corp. (Osaka Branch)

Afternoon – flight to Tokyo

Sheraton Grande Tokyo Bay Hotel

Tuesday, March 29, 2005

Tokyo Disneyland (Summerson Family two-day break)

Wednesday, March 30, 2005

Tokyo Disney Sea

7:10 p.m. – Check-in at airport

9:40 p.m. – Flight NW22 Depart Tokyo

Wednesday, March 30, 2005

8:40 a.m. – Arrive Honolulu

Sheraton Waikiki

Thursday, March 31, 2005

9:05 p.m. – Check-in at airport

11:05 p.m. – Flight NW90 Depart Honolulu

Friday, April 1, 2005

6:14 a.m. – Arrive Los Angeles (LAX)

10:23 a.m. – Flight NW330 Depart LAX

5:49 p.m. – Arrive Detroit International Airport

Limousine home

CHAPTER 8: IAMZUMN 40

"Some things to think about"

When driving I have two rules: #1 – make sure I don't hit anyone, #2 – make sure nobody hits me. (This is especially helpful when driving in countries that have cars with the steering wheel on the right side of the car.)

When traveling: You can always eat, but you can't always see. Take the time to see first.

When it comes to time I spend in the car by myself, I use the car as a mentor mobile – an educational environment utilizing time to get new thoughts, ideas, insights, information, and to "drink" from the thoughts of my mentors. It is a great way to "read" (listen to) a book and to leverage your already busy day. (Refer to the IAMZUMN website for my log of must listen to material.)

When it comes to reading: It is a choice. All of us have 15 minutes a day to read. Do it, NO EXCUSES. The books you read and the people you meet will make the difference in how you build your life.

When it comes to money: Spend less than you make and keep your money moving to ensure that it grows. Be generous in supporting others. Give 10 percent to your local church. Take charge of your money management.

When it comes to taxes: Pay your fair share.

When it comes to communication: #1 – Tell the truth. #2 – Keep your cool (even if you have had a bad day and the other person is wrong), #3 – Smile (your face reveals more about you than you think). #4 – Make eye contact (along with your smile), #5 – Be Fair. #6 – Understand that you can't make everybody happy.

When it comes to your living area and work place: Keep it clean and organized; something to be proud of – it is where you spend most of your time. Keep in mind the saying, "a cluttered desk is a cluttered mind."

When it comes to movies: Be discriminating. Our family loves to watch the classics; we can't get enough of "great" movies (a challenge to Hollywood); subscribe to NetFlix. Let the movies make me laugh, make me cry, make me sing, make me tough, make me feel pain. May they take me to the mountain top and make me sweat because what one watches does matter!

When it comes to music: I love classical violin, harpsichord, and symphony; I love rock and roll. I love popular music and even rap, too. I like musicals. I like movie themes. I like music loud and I like it soft. I like music both fast and slow. I love it when music makes me dance, I love it when it makes me feel emotion (such as *When a Man loves a Woman*). My son's criterion is "Louder is better" (Hmm?) When it comes to your life's work: Do it with gusto. "Play hard" – try to blur the line between work and play; personally, it helps me to enjoy living. Nevertheless, do what you love!

When it comes to my attitude in life: Being "in the zone" is natural, especially when my family lets me be extra enthusiastic in the morning. I believe it comes from within. It is a choice. Not everyone is as enthusiastic in the morning, but that doesn't mean that it is wrong for you. Your approach to life matters so let the enthusiasm of a child come from within and let it out....YES!!!

When it comes to raising children: Give your children your time – that is the currency of love. Be a part of your child's life – their time at home is too short for you not to!

When it comes to your thought process: Be more concerned about your outcome, not your "to-do" list; try, Anthony Robbins' R.P.M. Stop the stinkin' thinkin'! Understand that making the right decision determines your quality of life.

When it comes to recording your life: Take lots of pictures and organize them. Take lots of video. Record your thoughts in a journal; make it yours. This is your life and these are your memories and your friendships. Enjoy the process.

When it comes to God and Spirituality: Faith in Christ is first, supported with prayer. There are no second chances – when you are dead, you're dead.

Philippians 4:10-13 and 19 – "I rejoice greatly in the Lord that at last you have renewed your concern for me. Indeed, you have been concerned, but you had no opportunity to show it. I am not saying this because I am in need, for I have learned to be content whatever the circumstances. I know what it is to be in need, and I know what it is to have plenty. I have learned the secret of being content in any and every situation, whether well fed or hungry, whether living in plenty or in want. I can do everything through him who gives me strength. And my God will meet all your needs according to His glorious riches in Christ Jesus."

When it comes to mentoring: Give yourself permission to be mentored by someone. Some of my mentors have been – my parents, Dr. Stanley F. and Esther N. Summerson, business mentor and father-in-law Dr. Daniel R. Stewart, Paul Sobb (my accountant), Bruce Cramer (my attorney), Marnix Welvaert (my Belgian customer & friend), authors Jim Rohn, Denis Waitely, John Maxwell, Brian Tracy, Loral Langemeier, Napoleon Hill, Earl Nightingale and the list continues.

When it comes to personal growth: Take the high road and embrace your experiences and strengths. Learn, learn, learn, experience, experience, experience, and share what you can.

When it comes to you: Enlighten self interest (advice of Jim Rohn), not selfish interest – there is a difference.

When it comes to making a difference: I am the one to make a positive difference in people's lives.

When it comes to goals: Live in the moment and plan for the future. It is the process, the challenge to do great things.

CHAPTER 9: INTEGRITY:

"It's Your Decision"

Several years ago, I attended Jim Rohn's three day seminar in Anaheim, CA. One of his special guest speakers was Charlie "Tremendous" Jones who wrote the book *Life is Tremendous*. Charlie is a huge man who likes to give hugs. He opened his speech with his famous statement that <u>"your future will be affected by the people you meet and the books you read"</u>, and repeated that phrase many times during his speech: "the people you meet and the books you read." Today I believe that statement more than ever:" the people you meet and the books you read." As I look back at my life, the thoughts and ideas of people have changed my life.

When I was attending Mount Vernon Nazarene College (University), there were significantly less buildings on the campus. The MPB and the Cougar Den were the main places for campus activities. During my first year as a student, construction on Regents Hall was in its final stages. It seemed to rain six out of seven days during the fall, and I attended Calculus with Dr. Kauffman the first thing in the morning five days a week. It is a good thing that I am a morning person. As we entered the winter, the weather was harsh and there was so much snow and ice, the City of Mount Vernon was closed down and so was the college. The typewriter was one of the "must haves" in college. We didn't use e-mail and cell phones to communicate. I broke my right arm the last day of my junior year before exam week. During the summer I transitioned from typewriter to computer to type my senior paper during summer school using my left hand and my right-hand index finger. The computer I used was a dual floppy, no hard drive, mono color, single unit NCR machine. Reebok was the up-and-coming public offering. The junk-bond kings were Michael Milken and Ivan Boskey on Wall Street. The Shuttle Challenger exploded after lift-off, and in 1987 the movie Wall Street hit the screens starring Charlie Sheen as Bud Fox and Michael Douglas as Gordon Gekko who declared to the world that "GREED IS GOOD." During that same year I switched majors from pre-Med to business administration, enjoyed driving my burnt-orange Toyota Supra sports car, and met Karen – who later became my wife. Times were good except for Black Monday in October 1987 when the stock market crashed.

As I think about today and how technology has greatly changed, I am reminded how many things remain the same. Today we have similar problems with different names and stories. Instead of Milken and Boskey, we have Enron and World Com. Instead of NBC, ABC, CBS, we have CNN and FOX and any number of news shows on cable. Instead of Johnny Carson, it is Jay Leno. Instead of Billy Graham and Pat Robertson, we have Rick Warren and "The Purpose Driven Life" and Joel Olsteen's "Your Best Life Now." Instead of Atari, we have XBOX and Game Cube. My son Brian J. masters the computer games. Instead of Ford and GM we are seeing Toyota and Honda emerging as the big automakers.

Today we are living at a faster pace with more information to process. The Internet is used as a great business tool and now we have businesses that use this tool to promote their agendas globally. Every junior-high and high-school student is aware of myspace.com. It is a large 45,000,000 plus web community that enables people to be connected with others to share their pictures, thoughts, philosophy, and way of life. It is no longer "out there." It is "right here" with a click of a mouse. It is now PDA's, video Ipod, and video cell phones. It even affects my 14 year old. With the advent of blogging and "porn-to go" on cell phones, we now are subject to more pictures, opinions, information, and frustration. **In this fast-paced world, how can we live lives of integrity when we have so many distractions?**

What is Integrity? How do we get it? Do we need it? What are ethics? Why do we need to be so ethical?

What is Integrity?

Webster defines it as: adherence to moral and ethical principles; soundness of moral character; honesty.

What is being Ethical?

Webster defines it as: pertaining to or dealing with morals or the principles of morality; pertaining to right and wrong conduct.

What is being Moral?

Webster defines it as: of, pertaining to, or con cerned with the principles or rules of right conduct or the distinction between right and wrong; ethical; moral attitudes.

These moral attitudes have permeated all aspects of life. We have the Moral Majority, the Moral Philosophy, the Moral Rearmament, the Moral Sense, the Moral Theology, and the Moral Turpitude, or immoral conduct. The Bible has a collection of moral stories of people who did things right and did things wrong. The United States Congress passed the Sarbanes-Oxley Act of 2002 to guide moral business behavior. Even Felix Adler, in 1876, saw a need to guide moral behavior and established the New York Society for Ethical Culture.

Why is this so important?

As human beings, in order to live in a society together, we need an accepted and understood way to behave. For example: in the United States, we have agreed to drive our cars on the right-hand side of the road when the street is a two-way street. With this agreement, we have implicit trust that other drivers will "behave in the agreed upon manner." To deviate from this arrangement may and often does cause traumatic results. It is our responsibility to abide with this trust.

Webster defines trust as: the reliance on the integrity, strength, ability, surety of a person or thing; confidence; the confident expectation of something; hope.

Trust is also the foundation of all relationships. If I have trust in you, our relationship will flourish. If we do not have trust in the relationship, we will have problems. We trust in God. We trust that the President of the United States will make the right decisions. When we purchase stock in a company, we trust that the Board of Directors and company executives will manage the company for shareholder profitability instead of self interest. We trust the U.S. Postal Service to deliver our mail on time. I trust that you will respect human life and will not kill me. We trust that you will tell the truth. We trust that when we play sports together, you will play fairly. These agreed expectations, or guidelines, if you will, have evolved through discovering how to do things right and/or wrong as we figure out how to live and behave in this world. We know that humans are bent toward breaking this trust. In Exodus, we are given the Ten Commandments, <u>not suggestions</u>, to help us live better lives as persons in the community. God knew what we needed.

Your behavior at home, school, church, and in the market place does matter. Ultimately you will be held accountable.

The prerequisite to living a life of integrity is to <u>want</u> to live a life of integrity.

Let me repeat that statement: **The prerequisite to living a life of integrity is to <u>want</u> to live a life of integrity.**

As I have traveled around the world, I have met many good people. For the most part, people are living their lives believing they are good people. If you read the paper or listen to the media, it appears that a lack of morals and ethics is the rule, not the exception. Each culture has its own way of living, laws, and customs. Even in our culture, there is still an unwritten code to live by.

My experience of living in the United States is very different than living in other countries of the world. In March 2005, I took my son Brian on a business trip around the world. One of the countries we visited was India. Doing business in India can be challenging. During my visit, my customer, Mr. Sarin, arranged a private car to take my son and me to see the Taj Mahal. With in the first hour and a half of the drive, I noticed I was clenching my jaw as a response to my driver negotiating our path at a high rate of velocity through chaos on the road to Agra. My rules and the laws I live with are different than theirs. I prefer safety and consistency when driving – not what appears to be chaos and life threatening. I now know and understand a little more about their culture and can adjust my sensitivity to their behavior in our culture. Does this make it right? Does it make it wrong?

Is it right that we in the United States can use Benadryl (with pseudoephedrine), but in Australia it is considered a controlled substance? Do I carry Benadryl when traveling into Australia because it can help save my son from an allergic reaction? It is an ethical dilemma. If I do take the drug into Australia, I would be breaking its law and, if caught, I would have to pay a fine. From our point of view, the drug is acceptable. The Australian government has a different point of view.

In the first example I have given about traveling in India educated me that my experiences differ from others and the same situation can have many different points of view. The second example, about carrying Benadryl, shows that some laws create ethical dilemmas when other governments are involved.

Experience has shown that when people have made a conscious decision to win, that decision increases their odds greatly that they <u>will</u> win.

Think about how you may respond to me if I said Let's play Simon Says." (refer to Anthony Robbins seminar)

You may have thought casually, "sure, I can play Simon Says;" or "I am tired;" or "That's a kid's game" or "Do I have to?"

Or you might have thought "Simon Says, I love that game and I am going to win."

Think about it.

Winners make conscious decisions.

Let us apply that to the real world…

If you casually go about your business life and do not give much thought about your integrity, how will you conduct your decision making? You probably will make lots of mistakes, cut the corners and lose sight of the BIG

PICTURE. Do we know anyone like that? Maybeeeee, like Martha Stewart – one bad decision cost hundreds of millions of share-holders' dollars and five months of her life...for what? To her – pennies of profit. She blew it!

In the book *Naked in the Boardroom*, Robin Wolaner has a list of truths, as follows:

> Truth #32: When the stakes are enormous and the pressure is intense, even a normally-ethical person can make a mistake.
>
> Truth #30: You can learn and benefit from others' ethical lapses.

For those of you who will make a conscious choice to be men and women of integrity, your chances of making better decisions increases – and with the help of God and his principles, He can help you through the very, very tough times and, believe me, they will come. We are all human beings and "the world" attacks the good.

The point is this: the world is full of people who are not like you, who are not raised like you, who do not believe like you, who do not desire like you, and who do not think like you. All of us are being influenced daily by the popular cultural trends – movies, politics, advertising, internet, religion, and news.   In 1981 when I was in high school, MTV hit the airwaves. REO Speedwagon, Journey, Rush, Michael Jackson and Madonna were popular. Today, MTV has moved from music to lifestyle – they are masters at marketing it.

Even Pepsi has a great ad showing the power of influence that was aired during the 2004 Super Bowl:

> P. Diddy was on his way to the Award ceremony and his limousine broke down. A driver of a Diet Pepsi truck stops and gives P. Diddy a lift. When P. Diddy arrives at the awards ceremony, he climbs down from the truck. People in the crowd react when he makes an appearance. Later, you see people – the ones who were influenced by his arrival in the "diet-Pepsi truck" – driving their fashionable diet-Pepsi trucks.

Great commercial.

The 2005 Diet-Pepsi Super Bowl commercial with the help of P. Diddy, now is selling Brown and Bubbly.

Power of Suggestion:

If I tell you that you are confident, and continued to

tell you that you are confident, chances are that you will feel confident. If I tell you it is okay to steal from your employer, you would, **I hope**, probably respond that it is not okay to steal from your employer. However, if you pad your expense account because "no one will know," you are stealing from your employer. If you say "no one will know" over and over in you mind, it will shift your thinking from right to wrong. This is faulty thinking and creates the foundation to cut corners when the big ethical decisions come about.

Because of this, we have to be on our guard every day 24/7. We are instructed in Ephesians 6:13 to put on the full armor of God, so that when the day of evil comes, we will be able to stand our ground.

You will have an impact on the world around you. How well will you perform?

What is your reputation going to be?

I suggest striving to become a person of influence who has a foundation of integrity.

CHAPTER 10: IAMZUMN

"WILL YOU BE THE ONE?"

My hope in writing this book is to give a timeless gift to each person. For those contemplating doing more to build a great life, my goal is to inspire him or her to begin a journey that will enable personal growth, and to impact not only his or her life, but also enrich the lives of other people worldwide.

May you always seek guidance from the Lord above and live your life to positively impact the world. In the words of Zig Ziglar: "you can have everything in life you want if you will just help enough other people get what they want."

Today, your life has been a sum total of your thoughts and actions. All of us have been raised in some form of support (mostly in a family setting), given a genetic make up that determines our personalities and talents, experienced life-changing circumstances, and succeeded or failed. We are human beings.

My experience in life will be different than yours. Take a few minutes and write down in a journal or in the back of this book some of your life experiences. This exercise is a good beginning to understand what you have experienced and with this you can change to create a new and different experience.

Good fortune came my way all those years ago. Making the choice to become an entrepreneur was a risky proposition. What if I fail? What if I succeed? You may ask yourself do I really want to start a business. Yes, if that is what you truly desire. Taking action now and not waiting is part of the formula.

In 1989, I became employed as the bookkeeper of Dura Temp Corporation at age 22. Eleven months prior to taking the entrepreneurial route (1994), I was severely depressed and hated my accounting job. Can you relate? What if I had quit? On June 30, 2003 I "retired" – as defined by the general population - at the age of 36. My choice to stay at Dura Temp was one of my best decisions.

Life as an entrepreneur has provided me with life changing experiences that have made me grow and develop as a person, father, husband, leader, and business owner.

It has been hard work and I've made a lot of sacrifices. However, the rewards outweigh the difficulties. No one can guarantee that success will come your way, but I can guarantee that your life will be changed and you will learn through your successes and failures of your experience. I invite you to begin. Start small, what do you have to lose? I challenge you to go for it! I am glad **I** did. Becoming financially fit is an incredible ongoing education. This education allows me to continually grow as a human being all because I said "yes" to the call of entrepreneurship, thus ultimately leaving the life of living paycheck to paycheck. WILL YOU BE THE ONE!

www.IAMZUMN.com

www.MillionaireStrategist.com

www.DuraTemp.com

Remember to buy in GLASS!

ABOUT THE AUTHOR

Brian Thomas Summerson is the CEO of Dura Temp Corporation (www.duratemp.com), and founder of Summerson Capital Management, Inc. He has traveled to more than 40 countries and enjoys business strategy, traveling, investing, and reading. He and his wife, Karen, son, Brian (J) and their four Cairn Terriers, Heather, Nacho, Enchilada, and Lucky Girl live in Holland, Ohio.

Where in the world am I?